Copyright © 1997 by Wesleyan Publishing House
All Rights Reserved
Published by Wesleyan Publishing House
Indianapolis, Indiana 46250
Printed in the United States of America
ISBN 0-89827-178-9

All scripture quotations are from the HOLY BIBLE, NEW INTERNATIONAL VERSION ®. NIV ®. Copyright © 1973, 1978, 1984 by International Bible Society. Used by permission of Zondervan Publishing House. All rights reserved.

All rights reserved. No part of this publication may be reproduced, stored in a retrieval system, or transmitted in any form or by any means — electronic, mechanical, photocopy, recording or any other — except for brief quotations in printed reviews, without the prior written permission of the publisher.

Surprise Your Parents With A Call

1

Pick up the phone and call your mom or dad at work to tell them you love them. Don't ask for anything, just wish them a great day.

Make A Card

Using your own ideas, make a special card for your parents. Draw a picture of them on the front cover. Write mushy stuff inside . . . they like that kind of thing.

Sing Around The Home

Hum tunes you've learned at church or on the radio that are fun and upbeat. It will bring a joyful tone to the home and everybody will feel better because of your happy spirit.

4. Read To Your Brother Or Sister

If you have a younger sibling, read a book to him or her so your parents can have a free moment to work on something else. You'll be helping your parents and your brother or sister will love spending time with you. Let them pick out the book and turn the pages as you read. Have some fun making up voices for the different characters.

Call Your Grandparents

5

Surprise your grandma and/or grandpa with a phone call to say "I love you." Thank them for all they do for you and your parents. Tell them how glad you are that they had children so you too could be born.

6 Practice Ephesians 6:1

"**C**hildren, obey your parents in the Lord, for this is right." Be thankful if your parents are Christians and are teaching you to love the Lord.

Say "Thank You"

Parents do so much to serve us! Be thankful for the big and little things they provide. Thank them for your clothes. Thank them for a bed to sleep in. Thank them for loving you. Don't just think it, say it to them.

8 Be Helpful At The Grocery Store

Make it easy for Mom and Dad to shop. Don't pester them for things or grab items off the shelf. Instead, ask if you can help to find certain items on the shopping list or offer to push the shopping cart.

Look To Serve

Look for ways to help your parents at home. Pick up things on the floor. Put trash in the wastebasket. Wash off the counter. Put the lid down on the toilet — and don't forget to flush! Ask your parents how you can help with the housework.

Set A Standard

Do what is right and good. Even if other kids do bad things or try to influence you, don't give in to the pressure. If you set a good example in this way, you will help teach your parents how to live good, strong Christian lives, too.

11 Find A New Way Every Day

Watch for opportunities to be nice to your parents every day. Find a new way to encourage them each day for one week. They will love it.

Respect Your Parents

The Bible states in Leviticus 19:3, "Each of you must respect his mother and father . . ." This means you should be courteous and respectful to them. In other words, even if you don't agree with them, you must still speak kindly and in a way that honors them. Don't yell or throw a temper-tantrum. Remember, your parents are responsible for you until you are old enough to be on your own.

13 Write A Poem

Mom and Dad will love it if you make up a poem about them. Write it on a piece of white paper and brighten it up with colorful designs. They'll probably want to put it on the refrigerator or take it to their office, so act surprised if they do.

Go On A "Dollar Tree" Spree

When you're out shopping with your mom and dad, look for one of those stores that sells everything for $1.00. Take them into the store, tell them to pick out anything they want, and then buy it for them. Pretend you're the parent and they're the kids. (Be sure to use your own money.)

15 Sweep The Floor

If you see "stuff" on the floor (dirt or dustbunnies, cracker crumbs or dog hair), get a broom and sweep it up. If you know how to run the vacuum cleaner, tackle the carpet, too. Ask Mom if you can do this for her for a month. And then, if she says yes, don't forget to do it!

Don't Fight

Nothing frustrates parents more than when children fight. Try to keep peace in the home by having a positive attitude. Speak nicely to your brothers and sisters. If things get tense and you can't deal with it, ask permission to go to your room to settle down.

17 Make Good Choices

Proverbs 10:1 says, "A wise son brings joy to his father, but a foolish son grief to his mother." This verse teaches us that parents are happy when their children make good choices by obeying the Lord. They are disappointed and sad, however, when their children make bad choices. For both of your sakes, make good choices.

Ask Yourself: What Do They Think?

18

Think of some people at your school or in your neighborhood who know you. If they were asked to describe what you are like, what would they say? Live your life in such a way that people will say positive things.

19 Declare A Tickle War

Ask your parents if they will lie down on the floor and let you try to keep them down. Once they're all stretched out . . . start tickling them. They'll probably tickle you back, so be ready. Laugh and laugh and laugh together!

Leave Surprises Under The Pillow

20

Put a special surprise under your parent's pillow before you go to bed. Just a little note, or something you've made for them. Tell them to be careful because there might be something scary under their pillow. (This will give them a hint to look!)

21

Help Cook

Ask Mom or Dad if they would like you to help prepare the food for dinner. Make sure you wash your hands before helping, and be careful around the stove. They might even let you have some samples as you work together!

Get The Newspaper

22

After dinner, if your parents like to read the paper, get it for them. Ask them to relax in their favorite chairs and read while you take the dishes to the sink. Do as much of the cleanup as you can. Your parents will be thrilled.

23 Obey Your Parents

It's one of the TEN COMMANDMENTS (Exodus 20:12). Of course, we know that we should obey, but sometimes it's hard when parents have made a rule or a decision that you don't like. But it is the right thing to do and, according to this scripture, will bring blessings to your life.

24

Say "I Love You"

Say it before they do. Add little things to the sentence like "I love you . . . because you provide meals and 'stuff' for me." Think of the things your parents do for you and express your love to them.

Keep Your Clothes Picked Up

Put your dirty clothes where they belong. Ask your parents for a hamper for your room, or take dirty clothes to the laundry area without being told. When you come home and run to your room to change, take time to neatly put your clothes where they belong.

26 Make Your Bed

When you wake up, take time to straighten your bed before you leave the room. Not only will it be ready for you in the evening, but your mom or dad won't have to remind you to make it up or do it themselves. Once in a while your mom will want your sheets taken off to wash them. Ask her when you can help with that chore.

Don't Ask For Money

27

Save your money so you don't have to ask your parents for money every time you want to buy something. Surprise them by having money on hand the next time you're at the store. And if you're headed out with friends, tell your parents you don't need any money, and that you've saved up for this.

28 Love 'Em Like You Said

It's easier to *say* "I love you" than to *show* it. Really seek to love your parents with all your heart. Let them *feel* loved because of your obedience or servant spirit.

Do Your Chores

If you don't have a chore list, suggest a list of things you could do to help around the house — and don't just pick the easy stuff! Check off the weekly and daily things that are listed. If you *do* have a chore list, do each thing promptly — and throw in an extra chore for good measure.

30

Kiss And Hug

• • • • • • • • • • • • • • • •

Parents love to feel their children's arms around their necks. There's nothing more special than a free hug or kiss. Go give your parents one or two right now!

Don't Think Of Self *(except when renting videos)*

● ● ● ● ● ● ● ● ● ● ● ● ● ● ● ● ● ●

Try to make decisions that aren't selfish. For example, if your family is going out to eat, suggest going to the place your parents like to go. This will really surprise them. Try to put others before yourself — except when renting videos. The children's videos you like are the best ones for the whole family.

32 Love Your Brother And/Or Sister

God gave you siblings to love and enjoy. Even though you sometimes get frustrated with them, look for their good qualities and praise them for those qualities. If you don't have a brother or sister, "adopt" someone you know who needs to feel loved and appreciated.

Don't Interrupt Your Parents

33

● ● ● ● ● ● ● ● ● ● ● ● ● ● ● ● ●

When they're talking to other people, don't interrupt them with questions or comments unless it's an absolute emergency. When you interrupt, it drives your parents nuts!

34 Clean Your Plate

Your parents work hard to provide food for you. Even though some meals probably aren't your favorite things to eat, always try to be thankful and do your best to eat everything on your plate. After every meal, make it a habit to hug mom and/or dad and tell them thanks.

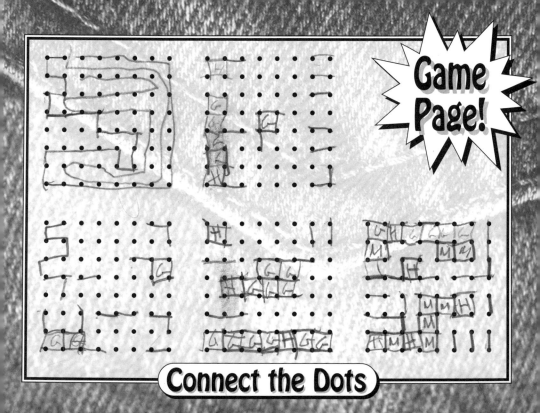

35 (For Boys Only) Never Hit Girls!

Learn to respect all ladies and girls. Never hit them or threaten them in any way. Treat them with kindness and respect.

Wash Your Hands

36

When you come in from playing outside or if you've been working on a dirty project, take time to wash your hands before running through the house. Otherwise you will leave dirty little fingerprints everywhere and someone (you know who) will have to clean them up.

37

Tell The Truth

Liars never win. It may look like it sometimes, but they never do. *Always* tell the truth, even if you have to suffer for it. You will soon be trusted by almost everyone when they know you tell the truth.

Fasten Your Seat Belt

Make it a habit — it's a proven lifesaver. Not only will you keep your parents from getting into trouble with the law, but you will prove to them how responsible you are.

39 Help With Yard Work

If you're old enough, offer to help with the yard work. Surprise your parents by having some of the outside chores done when they arrive home from work. Pull weeds. Pick up trash or twigs. Tidy up the garage.

Be Considerate Of Others

40

● ● ● ● ● ● ● ● ● ● ● ● ● ● ● ● ● ● ●

Think of your family members and their needs. Sometimes it helps to just sit quietly for awhile and think what you could do to "make their day." Then get up and do it!

Leave Love Letters

• • • • • • • • • • • • • • •

Put a love letter in your dad's lunch box or briefcase. Put one in your mom's purse or planner. They will be very surprised and pleased that you took time to do such a beautiful thing for them.

Laugh On Long Trips

42

Complaining and bickering on long trips only makes the trip drag on. Be sure you help everyone enjoy the trip by creating your own fun games or taking along some books to read.

43

Laugh On Short Trips

When you're just going for a short drive, don't argue over which seat you want or the best way to get there. Your parents are probably thinking about where they've got to go and what they've got to do. Help them out by being cheerful.

Stay Out Of Their Room

44

Sometimes parents want to be left alone in their room. Respect their privacy and let them enjoy their time alone together. Go to your room and enjoy having your own time of privacy. (Parents . . . you owe me for this one!!)

45

Don't Compare

• • • • • • • • • • • • • • •

Have you ever really liked something that your friend has and wished you could have it? A lot of times when we compare ourselves to people who have more than we do, we start thinking we should have more, too. But most of us already have plenty and there are many people who would love to have as much as we do. Thank God for all you have!

Is It The Shoes?

In Ephesians 6:15 God teaches us to wear "spiritual" shoes of peace everywhere we go. Sometimes we like to wear slippers so we can slip them off and say what we want to say. Then we put them back on and act like we haven't done anything wrong. Do you wear this kind of slipper? If so, ask Jesus to help you wear his shoes of peace and tie them on every day.

47 Don't Play With Your Food

Sometimes it's fun to roll your peas over each other or see how big a pile you can get on one side of the plate. And what mound of mashed potatoes isn't really a volcano in disguise, filled with hot gravy-lava? Moms especially don't like this and really appreciate it when you simply eat your food instead of playing with it.

Game Page!

```
C D O R S V F O A B C Y H A P P Y W
Z A H J T B N U M I P P L G S A W X
L D M O H E T V N W L X O U D K H E
E R V A B C M O R I A W Z I Q U A L
W E N F A M I L Y D Y M L S U V G K
Y P B E K T O C N D L O V U B R O C
W S U D A O Y R M P H A T W E Y L I
A D A C T I M O L C T H G A R O X T
N C A M P C K O M S G C R C T B U S
R V O I L T F A M S U T L U N C H A
```

FIND THESE WORDS:

FAMILY   MOM
HAPPY   LUNCH
VACATION   FUN
DAD   HOLIDAY
PLAY   TICKLE

Word Search

48

Sit Quietly

• • • • • • • • • • • • • • • • • •

At nice restaurants, in airports, in church, or wherever you have to just sit, parents love for you to sit quietly without disturbing others. Take a book along to read or a hand-held game to play. Or just enjoy watching the people around you.

Be Respectful Around The Phone

49

Show respect for your parents and the person they're talking to by not interrupting. Don't pick up another phone to ask your parent a question. Wait until they are off the phone and then talk to them.

50 Practice Love

God is love. When we love others and do things that are loving, we honor God. Love someone today by speaking kind words to that person or doing a kind deed.

Ask Jesus Into Your Heart

51

John 3:16 states, "For God so loved the world that he gave his one and only Son, that whoever believes in him shall not perish but have eternal life." The most important thing you will ever do is pray and ask Jesus into your heart. Simply believe He died for your sins and forgives you. Then you become His child and you will live with Him forever.

52

Be A Great Student

• • • • • • • • • • • • • • • •

Dedicate yourself to learning all you can. God has given you the ability to read these words and understand this sentence. What a blessing! Use the wonderful mind God has given you and fill it up with knowledge and wisdom.

Obey

53

Not only is it in the Bible and required by God, it's just good to do. If you learn to obey your parents, you will find obeying God is even easier.

54 Do Your Homework

Accept your assignments from your teacher with a good attitude. Discipline yourself to come home from school and do your homework before you play. Try to complete what you can during study hall or other free time at school.

Take Your Plate To The Sink

55

• • • • • • • • • • • • • • • • •

When you're excused from the table (don't forget to ask first and then say thanks), take your plate to the sink and volunteer to help clean up the kitchen. Offer your parents a day each week when you will clean up the kitchen by yourself.

56

Go To Sleep

When it's time to tuck away for the night, do it without a fight. You might prefer to stay up and watch TV or talk with a friend on the phone, but rest is important for your body. You will be more prepared for tomorrow if you know "when to say when."

Respect Your Parents' Privacy

Parents need time together every day. When they send you to bed or ask you to allow them time alone, respect their request and LEAVE THEM ALONE.

58 Play Outside

When possible, play outside. God has given us a beautiful creation to enjoy. Get out there. Be creative and invent new games . . . look under rocks for bugs, create some fun activities for the whole neighborhood, visit a nearby park (with permission), play football.

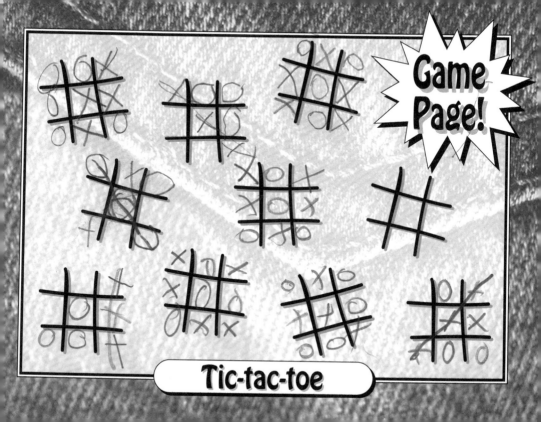

59 Don't Hog The Phone!

Especially if your family has only one phone line, try to limit your phone time. Tell your friends the best times to call. Check with your parents first to determine which times are best.

Wear A Coat

60

On cold, dreary days, put on a coat without being told and show your parents you know how to take care of yourself.

61

Flush!

. . . .

Come on . . . give us all a break!

Remember: You Are What You Eat

62

It's easy to fill up on candy and then not want dinner. If you do eat snacks or candy, be careful not to eat too much or you will ruin your appetite for good food. Eat healthy — you'll be glad you did.

63

Pray Every Day

Kneel by your bed at night and thank God for parents, friends, health, food, home and whatever else comes to your mind. Talk to Him and tell Him about the problems you're facing. He cares.

Be A Neighborhood Helper

64

Watch for ways to help out your neighbors. If there is an elderly person in your neighborhood, offer to get their mail or run errands for them. Busy moms and people with special needs will also benefit from your help. Serve them with a cheerful attitude.

65

Be Careful

••••••••••••••••••

Parents worry if they think you might do things that could be harmful or dangerous. Watch for cars when you're riding your bike or rollerblading. Always say a little prayer and ask the Lord to protect you.

Suggest An Activity

Offer an idea for a family fun time. Choose something that doesn't cost money but is fun. Here are some helpful ideas: bike rides, swimming, flying kites, playing ball, board games.

67 Teach Faith

• • • • • • • • • • • • • • • • •

God loves to hear the prayers of children. When you see how He answers your prayers, tell others.

Put On A Happy Face

68

When you smile, it makes everybody happy. Put one on right now and go show it off.

69

Pick Some Flowers

Give your mom or dad a bouquet of flowers. Do it on a day other than their birthday. Let it be a special day you make up. Call it "Because-I-Love-You" day. (Be sure you have permission to pick the flowers.)

Fix A Seat In The Sunshine

70

On a warm, sunny day, put a chair in the sunshine and find your mom and tell her you have a treat for her. Ask her what you can do to help her around the house and, as you do it, invite her to relax in the warm sun. If she's too busy, it's okay. She'll love the fact that you thought about her.

71

Make A Mom List

Make a list of all the things Mom does for you. At the top write "THANKS, MOM." Surprise her with it as you go to bed. She will think about you a lot that evening and it will end her day in a very special way.

ABCDEF
GHIJKL
MNOPQ
RSTUV
WXYZ

elephant

Game Page!

cute

ABCDEFGHIJKLMN
OPQRSTUVWXYZ

Hangman

72

Make A Daddy List

Do the same for Dad . . . he likes to be noticed too.

Memorize It

73

Get into the habit of memorizing Bible verses. It's good to have them in your mind because Jesus will use them to guide your life.

74

Live It

Don't just memorize Scripture, live it! A good place to begin is with the verse "Do to others as you would have them do to you" (Luke 6:31). Living this scripture will change the way you talk to and treat others. It is important for Scripture to get off the pages of the Bible and into your heart and mind.

Have A Piggy Bank Tank

75

Have a special place to keep your money. When you get ready to spend your money, be sure to save some and give a portion of it to God.

76

Give It Away

When a friend is over and likes one of your toys, give it to him or her. Everything you have belongs to the Lord and you will feel good when you brighten someone's day. (Be sure you let your parents know what you're doing first.)

Remember: Repetition Creates Reputation

77

It's normal for people to have opinions about you. They may say you're kind or you're funny or you're hardworking. The reason they have an opinion is because of the way you act. So . . . live and act in such a way that people have a good opinion of you. Be honest, loving, trusting — like Jesus.

78 Learn From Mistakes

All of us fail. When you do, don't get down and have a bad attitude. Instead learn from your mistake and try to live without making the same mistake again.

Soar Like An Eagle

79

The eagle was born to fly. A mother eagle disturbs the nest of her growing babies so they will learn to fly. As your parents give you more freedom, they are helping you learn to "fly." Be willing to accept these new challenges and soar like an eagle.

80 Don't Cry Wolf!

Remember the story of the little boy who kidded around about the wolf chasing him? Unfortunately, when the wolf really *did* chase him, no one believed him. Be sure others know when you are joking. Then when you are serious, people will believe you. But don't stop having fun, just be sure the time is right!

Moving?

81

If your parents decide to move, here are some helpful ideas. First, think about the positive side of the move. You will meet new friends, see new places and possibly have even more fun than you're having now. Second, even if the move will be tough on you, remember it might be a tough time for your parents too. Think of ways to encourage them as you prepare to move and even after you have moved.

82 Follow God's Heartbeat

When God made you, He had a special idea and plan in mind. You will make a difference for Him as you continue to love Him. Follow God and His "heartbeat" for your life.

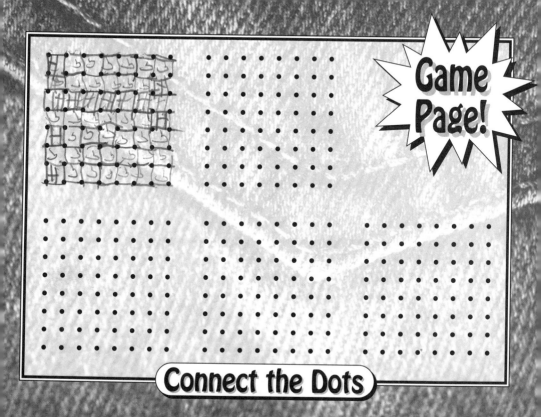

Game Page!

Connect the Dots

83

Be a "Start To Finish" Kid

Whatever you start, finish. If you start mowing the lawn, finish it. If you start washing the dishes, finish them. When you finish, look back and celebrate a job well done.

Invent Something

84

Think about all the things you do. Come up with an idea that will make it easier to perform one of those tasks. Share your idea with your parents or a teacher. This is a great way to exercise the awesome mind God gave you.

85 Whatcha Gonna Do?

If your parents don't show up to take you home from school? . . . if an accident happens and you're the only one who can help? Make sure you know phone numbers and addresses of people and places that can help you in an emergency situation. Talk with your parents and make sure you're prepared.

Forgive!

86

1 Corinthians 13 teaches us that one of the key ingredients of love is being willing to forgive. It says that love holds no grudges. When your parents, brothers, friends or others do something against you, forgive them and go on. You will understand Christ's love for you more as you practice the art of forgiveness.

87

Sit In God's Lap

••••••••••••••••

When you've had one of those "bad and ugly" days, go to your bedroom and sit on your bed. Close your eyes and imagine that God is holding you. Feel His arms of love comforting you. Talk to Him. No one cares for you more than God.

Give Three Hugs A Day

88

• • • • • • • • • • • • • • •

Parents love hugs. Give them three and they'll jump with glee. Tell them thanks for being awesome.

89

Don't Eenie, Meenie, Miny, Moe

Every day you make choices — some tough, some simple. Make sure you don't just "eenie, meenie, miny, moe" your choices. It other words, ask Jesus to guide you into right decisions with both the simple and the tough choices in life.

Fight Temptations

Ever since the beginning of time, Satan has tried to get us to fail. He did it to Adam and Eve and he will do it to us. The Bible says Jesus will give us the strength to make it through the temptations. (1 Corinthians 10:13) The next time you are tempted to do something wrong, stop and pray and push Satan away!

91

Make A Lasting Handprint

● ● ● ● ● ● ● ● ● ● ● ● ● ● ●

Make a print of your hands on a piece of paper or something you create especially for your parents. Write your name, your age and the date on the paper and give it to them. Ask them to put it somewhere special in the house or their office. They will always be able to see how big your hands were when you were this age.

Enough Is Enough

92

If your parents seem especially tired or edgy, don't pick on them . . . or your brothers or sisters. Sometimes they need a break! Give them one!

93

Shut The Gates

● ● ● ● ● ● ● ● ● ● ● ● ● ● ● ●

You have three major gateways into your life. Your eyegate (what you see), your eargate (what you hear), and your mouthgate (what you say). As the saying goes, "Hear no evil, see no evil and speak no evil." Look at what Christ would want you to see. Listen to what Christ would want you to hear. Say what Christ would want you to say. Let your gates praise the Lord.

Scratch Their Back

Ask your mom or dad if they will let you scratch their back. After you've rubbed or scratched for a little bit, put your arms around their neck and whisper in their ear . . . "I love you."

95 Mirror, Mirror On The Wall

Ever feel like you're not the prettiest or the smartest or the fastest or the bestest? That's reality, you *aren't*. You'll always find someone who can do things better than you. Stop fretting about it. Be thankful for who *you* are and focus on helping those who aren't as blessed as you. You'll soon forget your weaknesses as you exercise your strengths.

List The Top 5 Things You Like About Your Family

Top 5!

1.
2.
3.
4.
5.

96

Have Lotsa Fun

• • • • • • • • • • • • • • • • •

On a day when your family is in a happy mood, play a little trick on your mom and dad. Climb under their bed and when they come into the room, grab their legs and yell "Boo!" If they get mad, you can show them you read it in this book!

Look Forward... 97

To what you will do for God . . . to the joys of the next few days . . . to your next day off from school . . . to your next birthday . . . to ???

98 Practice Joy

There's nothing better than being joyful. Be joyful when your parents make decisions that you don't agree with. Be joyful when your family goes somewhere you would rather not go. It's your decision . . . TO BE JOYFUL.

Create A Course

99

Pick out several trees or poles in the neighborhood and make up a frisbee golf course. Decide what would be a fair par for each hole and invite the neighborhood to a fun game of frisbee golf.

100

Brush!

• • • • • • • • • • • • • • • • •

your hair or your teeth, maybe both. Do it without having to be asked.

Wake Up And Pray

101

Sometimes we wake up happy and sometimes grumpy. The grumpy times are hard on everyone. Take time to pray for yourself and your family before you get out of bed. Ask Jesus to help you have a joyful attitude every morning.

Top 10! YOUR 10 Favorite Ways To Be An Awesome Kid

1. Sweep the floor
2. Teach Faith
3. Clean your plate
4. Practis Jay
5. Obey your parents
6.
7.
8.
9.
10.